Barn Owl
(Tyto alba)

GW00647855

- Length: 33 - 35cms (13-14ins)
- Wingspan: 85 – 93cms (33 – 37ins)
- Weight: 0.24 – 0.36kg (8 – 13oz)
- Habitat: The greatest concentrations are found in low-lying arable areas near coasts where prey is abundant. The Norfolk coastal areas are ideal. The Barn Owl nests in hollow trees, buildings and crevices in rocks.

The Barn Owl was once a familiar sight in the British countryside. As its name suggests, it was frequently found in and near farm buildings, where it was welcomed by farmers because of its usefulness in pest control.

Unfortunately, as 20th Century farming methods led to the destruction of hedgerows, meadowland and field headlands – with the consequential loss of habitat for prey species – and as old farm buildings were either demolished or converted to other uses, the Barn Owl population crashed to a dangerously low level. At the turn of the 21st Century it was estimated that there were less than 4,000 breeding pairs left in Britain, a number which has fluctuated within a narrow parameter since.

The Barn Owl's prey consists mainly of small mammals, in particular short-tailed and field voles, mice and common shrews. These it either still-hunts from a perch or searches for by quartering over meadowland, often hovering, with moth-like silent fluttering flight as it relies on its superb hearing to locate prey.

It is estimated that a pair of Barn Owls and their young may eat about 1,000 rodents between them during the three-month breeding season.

Tawny Owl
(Strix aluco)

- Length: 37 - 39cms (14-16ins)
- Wingspan: 94 – 104cms (37 – 41ins)
- Weight: 0.3 – 0.58kg (11oz – 1lb 4oz)
- Habitat: Deciduous and mixed woodland but will live in farmland,
                 parks and even large gardens, provided there are trees and
                 prey. The Tawny usually nests in hollow trees.

The Tawny Owl (also known as the Hoot Owl and Brown Owl) is Britain's most numerous owl. This prevalence is largely due to its nocturnal habits, which have given the Tawny some protection from persecution. Also its size, physical dominance, varied diet and ability to adapt to changing circumstances and exploit new habitats such as urban parkland and even large gardens, have enabled it to sustain larger numbers. However, in recent years there has been concern that the UK breeding population of approx. 50,000 pairs may now be in gradual decline and is now Amber listed in conservation priority.

The Tawny has also been relatively unaffected by pesticide poisoning. Indeed the only major problem it has experienced is the loss of some nest sites following the spread of Dutch Elm disease and several years of severe winter gales.

Weighing up to 0.58kg and with a wingspan of up to 104cms, the Tawny is Britain's largest mainland breeding owl. The Tawny has an extremely varied diet which includes rodents, birds taken from night roosts and invertebrates. Some Tawny Owls have been known to take fish, frogs and other amphibians by wading in the shallows.

Little Owl
(Athene noctua)

- Length: 21 - 23cms (8 - 9ins)
- Wingspan: 54 – 58cms (21 – 23ins)
- Weight: 0.15 – 0.23kg (5oz – 8oz)
- Habitat: Little Owls prefer open country and avoid dense woodland. In Britain they favour agricultural land with plenty of hedgerows. Nests include holes in trees, walls and in the ground, including rabbit burrows.

The aptly named Little Owl is Britain's smallest owl, with a wingspan of less than 60cms and weighing only up to 230gms. But its aggressive expression, accentuated by pronounced eye ridges and a relatively undeveloped facial disk, makes this tiny predator appear fierce out of all proportion to its size.

For most of the year the Little Owl's diet consists mainly of large insects, earthworms and a few small mammals. However, during the breeding season, this is supplemented with small birds such as sparrows and thrushes.

Whilst the Little Owl is now native to Britain, it is only a recent arrival, having been introduced by man in the late nineteenth century. The first breeding success was recorded in Rutland in 1891 following the importation of a great many owls from Holland by Lord Lilford. Numbers grew rapidly and reached a peak in about 1930.

Since then, the population has declined, due largely to loss of habitat, pesticide poisoning, falling rates of juvenile survival and – because of its largely diurnal habits – persecution and collisions with road traffic.

Short-Eared Owl
(Asio flammeus)

- **Length:**   37 - 39cms (15 - 16ins)
- **Wingspan:**   95 – 100cms (37 – 40ins)
- **Weight:**   0.26 – 0.42kg (9oz – 15oz)
- **Habitat:**   Open country. Unlike other Owls, the Short-Eared builds its own nests, either ground scrapes in tall vegetation, or more substantial structures in wet areas.

Photo | Sander Meertins

Short-Eared Owls are unusual owls in their preference for open country, notably moorland, heathland, marshes and sand dunes. However, the population is extremely mobile and this – combined with its migratory habits – makes any estimation of their numbers very difficult, but has latterly been quoted by the R.S.P.B. as between 600 and 2,200 pairs and is Amber listed in conservation priority.

Despite being a specialist feeder on small mammals (especially voles), the Short-Eared Owl is very adaptable and will feed on a wide variety of other species during temporary slumps in the vole population. Its normal hunting method consists of quartering the ground at a height of less than 3 metres, alternating between flapping its wings and gliding, and occasionally hovering whilst searching for its prey.

Short-Eared Owls have a maximum wingspan of 1 metre, but weigh less than half a kilo. The very small ear tufts from which they get their name have nothing to do with hearing but are used to communicate mood to would-be aggressors.

Long-Eared Owl
(Asio otus)

- Length: 35 - 37cms (14 - 15ins)
- Wingspan: 90 – 100cms (35 – 39ins)
- Weight: 0.2 – 0.4kg (7oz – 15oz)
- Habitat: The Long-Eared Owl uses mainly small patches of woodland, especially conifer plantations. However, it avoids the centre of dense woods. This Owl will also use farmland, parks and even large gardens. It does not nest in holes, but uses abandoned nests of other birds such as magpie and crow.

Superb camouflage, an ability to alter its shape to blend with its surroundings (by fluffing-up or flattening its feathers), very nocturnal habits and a tendency to favour woodland habitat – all these factors make the Long-Eared Owl the least known of Britain's native owls.

The Long-Eared Owl's most prominent feature is the pronounced 'ear' tufts from which it derives its name. In most 'tufted' owl species (the Eagle Owl family, for example) these have probably nothing to do with hearing but are manoeuvred by the owl to reflect mood or to aid with camouflage. Nevertheless the Long-Eared Owl has remarkable hearing: its facial disc channels sound to complex and asymmetric ear openings which run nearly the full height of its skull. The muscles required to alter the position of the ear tufts are also thought to play a part in changing the shape of the ear openings and therefore, may well mean that in the case of the Long-Eared Owl the 'ear' tufts have a role to play in hearing that enables the owl to detect, locate and strike at prey with total accuracy, even in complete darkness.

During the breeding season the Long-Eared Owl relies mainly on mice and voles for its food, but during the winter will shift its feeding habits and place a far greater reliance on small to medium-sized birds. This trend is almost unique to the UK and happens in few other countries.

Eurasian Eagle Owl *(Bubo bubo)*

- Length: 66 - 71cms (26 - 28ins)
- Wingspan: 160 – 190cms (5ft 3ins – 5ft 11ins)
- Weight: 2 – 3.5kg (4lb 8oz – 7lb 15oz)
- Habitat: Open woodland in mountain foothills up to an altitude of 4,500m. Although sedentary, this large Owl requires a territory up to 10km in diameter. The Eagle Owl nests in ground scrapes usually among rocks.

The Eurasian Eagle Owl was a native of Britain until the latter part of the 19th Century and became extinct here largely as a result of man's persecution. In recent times reports of its return have become more frequent. One pair was known to breed in Scotland in the mid 1980s and another pair has been breeding in the north of England since 1996 and had raised 13 young by 2003. Lack of suitable habitat and our own reaction to them makes it unlikely they will ever return here in significant numbers.

Eagle Owls are the largest of the owls and their sheer size and aggressive nature makes them the dominant bird of prey (both nocturnal and diurnal) wherever they are found. Very occasionally they are killed by large eagles, but more often it is they who prey on other Raptors. The arrival of a new Eagle Owl in the vicinity causes panic amongst other birds of prey and a general re-arrangement of territories usually follows, as its new neighbours try to give it a wide berth.

Eurasian Eagle Owls prey mainly on mammals – chiefly rabbits and hares – but they will also take birds up to the size of a large buzzard, which are usually taken from night roosts. Large Eagle Owls have been known to take roe deer and foxes, which they kill by crushing their skulls with huge, powerful feet.

Photo | Ian Dyball

Snowy Owl
(Nyctea scandiaca)

- Length: 53 - 66cms (20 - 26ins)
- Wingspan: 142 – 166cms (60 – 65ins)
- Weight: 1.1 – 2kg (2lb 8oz – 4lb 9oz)
- Habitat: Arctic Tundra. British visitors favour mountains and moorland with short vegetation.

The Snowy is a large owl with a wingspan of around 1.5 metres. It can weigh up to 2 kilos and females are about 30% heavier than males.

The Snowy cannot be confused with any other owl because of its large body size, relatively small head and beautiful white plumage with dark speckles. Males are usually less marked than females.

The Snowy Owl enjoys a varied diet, often dependent on local prey availability. It takes rabbits, shrews and voles; birds, which can include geese, grouse and seabirds; and other birds of prey. Unusually for an owl the Snowy will also eat carrion.

The last record of Snowy Owls breeding in the UK was in 1967 on the island of Fetlar in the Shetlands, but this success only lasted until 1975 when the male disappeared leaving only a few females. Vagrant Snowy Owls do occasionally turn up in various parts of northern Scotland and have been sighted as far south as Lincolnshire.

The Snowy Owl's dense plumage – with feathers extending down to the toes – and its great bulk and compact shape, enable it to survive extremely low temperatures. The average winter temperature in the arctic tundra is -34°C!

Merlin
(Falco columbarius)

- Length: 25 - 30cms (10-12ins)
- Wingspan: 50 – 62cms (20 – 24ins)
- Weight: 0.12 – 0.30kg (4 – 11oz)
- Habitat: Open upland country. Hilly areas offer the best vantage points. Nests frequently in patches of heather. Some birds have taken to the forest margins.

The Merlin is Britain's smallest falcon with a maximum wingspan of only 62cms, but it is probably the most active. It does not stoop on its prey but chases it down in high-speed pursuit, rising above the prey at the last instant to strike downwards with its talons.

Britain has the largest population of Merlins in Europe thanks largely to the management of the grouse moors. It is predominantly a ground nesting bird which preys largely on small birds, such as meadow pipits and skylarks and small wading birds from estuaries, but will also take insects.

Hobby
(Falco subbuteo)

- Length: 30 - 36cms (12-14ins)
- Wingspan: 82 – 92cms (32 – 36ins)
- Weight: 0.13 – 0.34kg (4 – 12oz)
- Habitat: Heath and downland, provided there are some tall trees for nesting. Hobbies do not build nests but use abandoned crow, magpie & sparrowhawk nests or even squirrel dreys.

The heath and downlands of southern Britain are at the northern edge of the Hobby's range although many more visit this country to breed between April and late August each year before returning to Africa for the winter.

The Hobby is an extremely active and dashing little Falcon which specialises in catching large insects and small birds, especially housemartins and swifts which it takes in high-speed, surprise attacks. Hobbies are particularly active at dusk and have even been known to hunt large insects and bats by moonlight.

Like most falcons, Hobbies do not build nests but instead take over the disused nests of other birds, mainly rooks, crows and magpies.

Kestrel
(Falco tinunculus)

- Length: 32 - 35cms (12-14ins)
- Wingspan: 71 – 80cms (28 – 32ins)
- Weight: 0.14 – 0.31kg (5 – 11oz)
- Habitat: Kestrels do not build their own nests but use holes and forks in trees, scrapes on the ground, ledges on cliffs & buildings and old nests of other birds. Because of this ability, Kestrels are able to exploit a wide range of habitat.

Despite being persecuted during the 19th century when gamekeepers virtually eliminated it from some parts of the British Isles, the Kestrel made a successful comeback thanks to its remarkable adaptability. It has learned to take advantage of new hunting areas such as roadsides and even town centres. It is also able to switch to different prey whenever occasional slumps in the vole population occur.

Although the Kestrel is a true Falcon, its flight-style, prey and method of hunting are far from typical. The Kestrel feeds mainly on small mammals – principally the short tailed vole – which it hunts by hovering, head into the wind; or which it spots from a perch.

Mature male Kestrels are easily distinguished from females, being a warm red-brown colour with a grey head and tail. The female is mainly brown with darker speckles and bars and is slightly larger with a wingspan of over 75cms.

Photo | Paul Sawer

Peregrine Falcon
(Falco peregrinus)

- Length: 36 - 48cms (14-19ins)
- Wingspan: 95 – 110cms (37 – 43ins)
- Weight: 0.58 – 1.30kg (1lb 4oz – 2lb 14oz)
- Habitat: Rocky crags both coastal and inland. Sometimes found in forested areas but more commonly in open country. No nests are built but eggs are laid directly onto rocky ledges and sometimes even on tall buildings.

The Peregrine has always been highly prized by falconers, but the practice of falconry declined with the introduction of effective sporting guns. Moreover, as the interests of the bird came into direct conflict with those of the game-shooter the Peregrine became subject to persecution. Although other raptor populations were able to recover when game-keeping was suspended during the two world wars, they continued to be victimised on the grounds they killed carrier pigeons.

The widespread use of organochlorine pesticides such as DDT severely affected many species of birds of prey but since their use was banned in the late 1970's the Peregrine population has been restored

Peregrines are exclusively bird-eaters who take their prey in flight, either binding to the victim after a short chase in level flight or – more often – by climbing above the prey and stooping at speeds of over 200 mph, striking with the hind talon and often with sufficient force to kill outright.

The Peregrine is the largest of Britain's breeding falcons (the larger gyrfalcon is an occasional, non-breeding, visitor). Female Peregrines have a wingspan in excess of one metre and can weigh close to 1.4 kilos, while males weigh about a third less, giving rise to their being called the tiercel.

Sparrowhawk *(Accipiter nisus)*

- Length: 28 - 38cms (11-15ins)
- Wingspan: 55 – 70cms (22 – 28ins)
- Weight: 0.11 – 0.34kg (4oz – 12oz)
- Habitat: Mixed woodland with some open spaces and paths. The Sparrowhawk has adapted to using urban parks and large gardens, especially during the winter. Nests are built in tall trees.

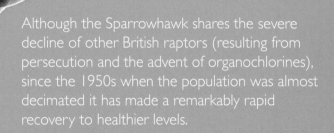

Although the Sparrowhawk shares the severe decline of other British raptors (resulting from persecution and the advent of organochlorines), since the 1950s when the population was almost decimated it has made a remarkably rapid recovery to healthier levels.

A rather small bird with short, broad wings, a long tail and long, slender legs, the Sparrowhawk is ideally suited to life in woodland.

The Sparrowhawk preys on small birds and uses its great agility to pursue its prey through woodland at high speed. However, it is sometimes so intent on its prey that it collides with trees and other obstacles: many are killed or injured in this way.

Sparrowhawks can carry prey as large as themselves (the female is 25% larger than the male, with a wingspan of up to 70cms) and will frequently take their kills to a favourite post to be plucked.

Goshawk
(Accipiter gentilis)

- Length: 48 - 62cms (18-25ins)
- Wingspan: 135 – 165cms (53 – 65ins)
- Weight: 0.62 – 2.05kg (1lb 6oz – 4lb 18oz)
- Habitat: Woodland (both deciduous and coniferous) with open glades and breaks for hunting. Nests in trees, sometimes refurbishing existing nests but, in conifer plantations, always building a new one.

In Great Britain the Goshawk was shot, poisoned and trapped to extinction during the 19th century by gamekeepers. Whilst it is true that the Goshawk is a formidable predator, most of this prejudice was based on an exaggerated opinion of its powers.

Of the two British species of true hawk (accipiters), the Goshawk is by far the largest being up to 6 times heavier than the Sparrowhawk. A large Gos can weigh over 2 kilos and have a wingspan in excess of 1.5 metres. It is predominantly a woodland bird and has adapted to living in conifer plantations where, to its great credit, the Forestry Commission actively protects known nest sites.

The Goshawk is completely fearless and will take quarry on the ground or in the air. It is capable of remarkable speeds over distances of up to 500m with deep, rapid beats of its comparatively short, broad wings.

Prey ranges from songbirds to hares. Victims are grasped with large, powerful feet and held with increasing pressure, driving in the long, sharp talons until all movement ceases.

Common Buzzard
(Buteo buteo)

- Length: 51 - 57cms (20-22ins)
- Wingspan: 113 – 128cms (44 – 50ins)
- Weight: 0.4 – 1.4kg (15oz – 3lb)
- Habitat: Buzzards build their nests in tress and sometimes on rocky ledges. When breeding they favour woodland with some open ground, but will also live on open moorland provided there are some trees.

The Common Buzzard is a medium sized raptor with a wingspan of more than a metre. Weighing up to 1.4kg, it has broad rounded wings and a fairly short tail which it uses to soar and glide effortlessly over hills and valleys. However, in direct flapping flight the Common Buzzard's movements can appear quite laboured and it prefers to still-hunt from a convenient perch, gliding down to seize prey in its talons.

The history of the Common Buzzard shows the usual pattern of persecution which drove it into western Britain, particularly the West Country, Wales and Scotland. During the late 1950s and early 1960s Buzzard numbers were dramatically reduced still further when myxomatosis wiped out over 90% of the rabbit population, so depriving it of its major source of food.

However, being an adaptable bird the Buzzard has since been able to exploit other sources of food including voles, young birds, reptiles, invertebrates and feeds widely on carrion.

The Common Buzzard has re-colonised much of its old territory and is once again amongst the most numerous of Britain's birds of prey.

Photo | Philip Berry

Honey Buzzard
(Pernis apivorus)

- Length: 52 - 60cms (20-24ins)
- Wingspan: 135 – 150cms (53 – 59ins)
- Weight: 0.4 – 1kg (15oz – 2lb 5oz)
- Habitat: Deciduous forest and mature pine & spruce woods, where bee and wasp nests are plentiful. The Honey Buzzard builds its own nest in tall trees and usually incorporates a mass of leafy twigs.

The Honey Buzzard is a migratory breeding visitor to Britain and is only present between mid-April and mid-August: winters are spent in Africa, south of the Sahara.

Although a frequent summer visitor to Europe, the Honey Buzzard is a very rare bird in this country – in 1988 there were records of only 10 pairs here, although – because it is a shy woodland bird – numbers have probably been under-recorded.

Despite its name the Honey Buzzard is not a honey eater at all but a specialised predator of wasp and bee larvae. It detects nests by observing the movements of insects whilst soaring or hovering above, and then digs out the larvae from the nest. The Honey Buzzard has special adaptations to cope with this particular food source. Scale-like feathers on forehead and cheeks protect it from stings whilst a long, narrow head enable it to investigate comparatively small holes in the ground: the Honey Buzzard's feet are adapted for digging, having short blunt talons and thick scales; and its nostrils are thin slits, less prone to being clogged with soil.

The Honey Buzzard can supplement its diet with small mammals, birds, eggs and invertebrates and will even eat fruit and berries.

Marsh Harrier *(Circus aeruginous)*

In addition
to the twin
hazards of
persecution and
toxic chemical attack
endured by our other
raptors, the Marsh Harrier
has been particularly affected
by habitat loss due mainly to land
drainage. Consequently the Marsh
Harrier effectively became extinct in Britain
in 1917.

During the following few years there were
occasional attempts by immigrant birds from Holland to
breed in the East Anglian reed-beds. However it was not until
1927 – when Lord Desborough, and later the Norfolk Naturalists'
Trust, gave them protection – that the population of Marsh Harriers
began its painfully slow recovery.

As its name suggests the Marsh Harrier is a wetland bird, usually
nesting in dense reed-beds or other thick vegetation in shallow water. It
feeds mainly on other marsh birds including duck and waders, but will
also take small mammals. Prey is usually caught by surprise as the Harrier
quarters the ground, using all available cover.

It is the largest of our Harriers, with a wingspan of well over one
metre and weighing up to 800gms.

Photo | Piotr Krześlak

- Length: 48 - 56cms (19 - 22ins)
- Wingspan: 115 – 130cms (45 – 51ins)
- Weight: 0.4 – 0.8kg (14oz – 1lb 12oz)
- Habitat: Wetlands where disturbance is minimal. Usually nests in large dense reed-beds, although some are now breeding on arable land.

Hen Harrier *(Circus cyaneus)*

During the breeding season, Britain's indigenous population of Hen Harriers is concentrated in Scotland, Ireland, Wales and northern England but during the winter the population disperses to coastal regions including East Anglia and south-east England.

The difference in appearance between the male and female Hen Harriers is striking, the males being a soft dove-grey with white rumps, and females having dark brown upper parts and yellow-brown underparts.

Along with many other British birds of prey, the Hen Harrier population declined drastically, partly due to loss of its heath, moor and marshland habitat. The population also shrank as a result of persecution by gamekeepers on grouse moors. It responded well to protection and habitat changes and numbers recovered. Unhappily, it is still under pressure from sporting interests who charge it with disturbing the game birds (mainly grouse) and killing their young.

With a wingspan of over a metre and weighing over half a kilo, the Hen Harrier hunts its prey of small mammals and ground nesting birds, by low-level systematic searching. For this it uses its superb hearing aided by an owl-like facial disk, and utilises all available cover to gain the advantage of surprise.

Photo | Dennis Jacobsen

- Length:
  44 - 52cms
  (17-21ins)
- Wingspan:
  100 – 120cms
  (39 – 47ins)
- Weight:
  0.3 – 0.7kg
  (10oz – 1lb 9oz)
- Habitat:
  Prefers open
  lowlands including
  bogs, moors, heaths
  and marshes but has
  adapted to young
  conifer plantations.
  Nests are always on
  the ground and in
  cover.

Montagu's Harrier
(Circus pygargus)

- Length: 43 - 47cms (17- 19ins)
- Wingspan: 105 – 120cms (41 – 47ins)
- Weight: 0.23 – 0.44kg (8oz – 1lb)
- Habitat: Lowland regions – marshes, sand dunes, young forestry plantations and heaths. More recently nesting in arable crops. Nests are always built on the ground, usually in tall vegetation including growing crops.

Of similar size to the Hen Harrier but more lightly built, Montagu's Harrier is the UK's rarest breeding raptor. It narrowly missed total extinction early in the 20th century at which time the population was confined mainly to the Norfolk Broads.

That the Montagu has survived at all is largely due to a shift from its normal habitat to the use of crop fields (mainly cereal) for nesting. Also, co-operation between farmers and conservation organisations has played a part. As a result the Montagu has established new territory in southwest Britain. A purely migrant visitor, present only between April and September, there have been years when no breeding pairs have appeared.

The diet of Montagu's Harrier is extremely varied and includes small mammals, songbirds, invertebrates, reptiles, amphibians and the chicks and eggs of ground-nesting birds. Normal hunting flight is a series of slow glides punctuated with strong, rapid wingbeats. This extremely buoyant bird is capable of rapid changes of direction and sudden stoops. Unlike other harriers, Montagu's can fly fast enough to chase fast-moving ground prey and can even take small birds in flight.

Photo | Mikalay Varabey

Red Kite
(Milvus milvus)

- Length:
  60 - 66cms
  (23-26ins)

- Wingspan:
  175 – 195cms
  (69 – 77ins)

- Weight:
  0.76 – 1.6kg
  (1lb 11oz – 3lb 8oz)

- Habitat:
  Roosting and nesting
  in valleys containing
  ancient oakwoods, but
  hunting over heath and
  moorland. Lowland
  pastures and wetlands
  are also used during
  the winter.

The Red Kite was once a common sight in British skies and during the Middle Ages was legally protected because of its practice of clearing human refuse from towns and cities.

Unfortunately, the Red Kite was also a major predator of domestic fowl and this led to its relentless persecution. By 1905 the total British population was reduced to only 12 birds.

The Red Kite is once again a protected species and, with birds imported from Sweden and Spain, a reintroduction scheme has successfully brought them back to many parts of England and Scotland, central Wales and central England - especially the Chilterns and the East Midlands.

With a wingspan of almost 2 metres, a slender body and long forked tail, the Red Kite is our most elegant bird of prey and one of the most skilled in flight. It will eat almost anything (dead or alive) and will often steal food from other birds of prey.

Photo | Paul McKenna

Osprey
(Pandion haliaetus)

- Length: 55 - 58cms (21-23ins)
- Wingspan: 145 – 170cms (57 – 70ins)
- Weight: 1.1 – 2kg (2lb 8oz – 4lb 8oz)
- Habitat: Coasts and near any lake, reservoir or river which is free from disturbance and where fishing is possible. Nests in trees and on artificial platforms.

Persecuted to extinction in Britain by 1917, the comeback of the Osprey started in 1959 when a pair bred successfully at Loch Garten in Scotland. This site - now under the permanent protection of the R.S.P.B. - attracts many thousands of human visitors each year.

The Osprey is a migratory bird which spends the winter in Africa, but when mature each year returns to breed.

Although it will sometimes feed on other small prey, the Osprey is a specialist fish-eater and will plunge into the water from about 10m, sometimes becoming completely submerged in its quest for food.

Ospreys' feet are specifically adapted to catch fish. They have long, sharp, very curved talons and the undersides of the feet are covered in tiny spikes. Ospreys are also able to turn their outer toes to the rear, so giving them two opposing pairs of talons. Among diurnal Raptors, this ability is unique.

Compared to a body weight of up to 2 kilos, the Osprey has very large wings with a span of up to 170cms. These it uses to lift both itself and its prey – both soaking wet – from the water's surface. The Osprey hangs in mid-air and after a few strong wing-beats to shed water and a characteristic shake of its body, flies off to feed.

Golden Eagle
(Aquila chrysaetos)

- Length: 75 - 88cms (30-35ins)
- Wingspan: 204 – 220cms (80 – 87ins)
- Weight: 2.8 – 6.7kg (6lb 3oz – 14lb 11oz)
- Habitat: Open mountainous land. Nests are huge structures of twigs and small branches on rocky ledges.

The Golden Eagle – its name is due to the golden crown and neck feathers – is Britain's only true or "booted" Eagle. With a wingspan in excess of 2 metres and weight which may be in excess of 6 kilos, it is Britain's second largest bird of prey after the White-Tailed Eagle.

The Golden Eagle is largely confined to the mountain regions of Scotland, where it uses the strong winds and updrafts to soar effortlessly in search of its food, consisting mainly of carrion, rabbits and hares. Here the population remains fairly stable – in 2003 a comprehensive survey found 431 pairs.

Apart from persecution and disturbance, the main threats still facing the Golden Eagle result from the use of land for conifer forestry, (which reduces the availability of prey) and improved methods of sheep husbandry, which has resulted in a significant reduction in carrion. The latter has greatest effect during the lean winter months when sheep are driven to more sheltered lowland pastures.

Photo | Andreanita

White-Tailed Eagle
(Haliaetus albicilla)

- Length: 68 - 90cms (27-36ins)
- Wingspan: 200 – 240cms (78 – 94ins)
- Weight: 3.1 – 6.9kg (6lb 13oz – 15lb 3oz)
- Habitat: Coasts and near large lakes and rivers, nesting as much as 10km inland. The White Tail builds huge nests of wood, heather and seaweed which may be 1.5 metres across.

In its adult form, the White Tailed Eagle has all the hallmarks of a classic Sea or Fish Eagle. It is a large, dark bird with a contrasting white tail; its legs are unfeathered; the beak is large and powerful, and it has a loud, high-pitched call.

Slightly larger than the Golden Eagle, the White Tailed Eagle has the greatest wingspan of any British bird, spreading to almost 2.5 metres. Females weigh about 25% more than males and can weigh almost 7 kilos. In flight, the White Tailed Eagle is easily distinguished from the Golden Eagle by its very short tail.

The White Tail was persecuted to extinction in the British Isles when, in 1918 the last survivor – an elderly female – was shot. Since then, some individuals have drifted to our shores but it was not until the late 1970s that they were successfully reintroduced from Norwegian stock on the Scottish Island of Rhum, with the first breeding success following in 1985.

The White Tailed Eagle is a coastal bird and, in this country, is limited to the Western Isles of Scotland although attempts are being made to re-introduce it to coastlines in southern and eastern England. It is an active predator, taking fish, mammals and waterbirds. It is also an eater of carrion and will steal food from other birds of prey and gulls.

An Introduction to
British Owls
and other
Birds of Prey

Clive Britcher

This book provides a compact reference to owls and other birds of prey which can be seen in the British Isles.

Alongside some stunning photographs, you will find specific information about the population, distribution, size, habitat and conservation status of each species.

Published by:
The Suffolk Owl Sanctuary
Tel: 03456 807 897
www.owl-help.org.uk

Suffolk Owl Sanctuary
Reg. Charity 1086565

9 781900 690003 >